WALKING CLOS

CW00394814

BURY ST EDMU

Number Twenty Four in the popular
series of walking guides

Contents

Walked, Written and Drawn by Clive Brown

Clive Brown 2004 – 2021

Published by Clive Brown
ISBN 978-1-907669-24-8

PLEASE
Take care of the countryside
Your leisure is someone's livelihood

Close gates
Start no fires
Keep away from livestock and animals
Do not stray from marked paths
Take litter home
Do not damage walls, hedgerows or fences
Cross only at stiles or gates
Protect plants, trees and wildlife
Keep dogs on leads
Respect crops, machinery and rural property
Do not contaminate water

Although not essential we recommend good walking boots; during hot weather take something to drink on the way. All walks can easily be negotiated by an averagely fit person. The routes have been walked and surveyed by the author, changes can however occur, please follow any signed diversions. Some paths cross fields which are under cultivation. All distances and times are approximate.

The maps give an accurate portrayal of the area, but scale has however been sacrificed in some instances for the sake of clarity and to fit restrictions of page size

Walking Close To have taken every care in the research and production of this guide but cannot be held responsible for the safety of anyone using them.

During very wet weather, parts of these walks may become impassable through flooding, check before starting out. Stiles and rights of way can get overgrown during the summer; folding secateurs are a useful addition to a walker's rucksack.

Thanks to Angela for help in production of these booklets

Views or comments?
walkingcloseto@yahoo.co.uk

24:

Walking Close to
Bury St Edmunds

The walks contained in this booklet make use of rights of way, paths, bridleways and long distance trails in the Bury St Edmunds area. There is very little walking on roads except where unavoidable. Most are on firm, good quality paths and well marked and signposted. Paths may cross fields under cultivation and some are more obscure and less well directed; the detailed instructions will guide past these points. Some of the walks are in areas popular with walkers already, others are in areas less popular and perhaps less accessible.

The town of Bury St Edmunds is situated off the A14 trunk road where the A134 is confusingly crossed by the A143. Originally the settlement of Beodericsworth, it was the eventual resting place of the remains of the Saxon King Edmund. He was born in 840 and crowned King of the East Angles in 855. During the 860's he had to deal increasingly with the threat of a Danish invasion. A large army led by Ivar the Boneless led a series of raids in 865, after forays to Nottingham and York he returned to East Anglia in the autumn of 869 to his winter camp in Thetford. On November 20th of that year Edmund lost the ensuing battle with Ivar; after his refusal to renounce Christianity he was used as target practice by Viking archers before being beheaded. The separated head which had been thrown into brambles was later found by a Saxon search party whose members agreed that they had been alerted to the head's location, being guarded by a wolf, by shouts of 'here'. They were unable to agree however whether the shout had been uttered by the wolf or the severed head. His tomb became a popular place of pilgrimage, prompting the town to change its name to Bury St Edmunds.

During the sugar beet 'season' the plume of smoke belching out of the chimney of the sugar beet factory marks its position for miles around. To travellers passing by on the A14, the ugly edifice of the sugar beet factory presents the wrong face to those who do not know the town. The cathedral is one of many impressive and historically important buildings in the town centre.

The maps give an accurate portrayal of the area, but scale has however been sacrificed in some cases for the sake of clarity and to fit restrictions in page size.

We feel that it would be difficult to get lost with the instructions and map in this booklet, but recommend carrying an Ordnance Survey map. All walks are on Explorer Maps Nos 210 & 211; Landranger No 155 covers at a smaller scale. Roads, geographical features and buildings, not on our map but visible from the walk can be easily identified.

adfield Woods

$2^3/_4$ Hours

~~ark at~~ Bradfield Woods, Grid ref TL935581, no toilets.

1   Walk away from the car park into the woods through the buildings; turn left at the first crossroads marked red/yellow/blue, turn right at the next post (same colours). Turn left again at the next marker, then right, along the inside edge of th wood. At post no 12, go straight on down the steps and over the footbridge.

2   Keep direction along the field edge, turn right at the end then left to regain direction. Just before the houses bear left down the path between the fence and the hedge, turn right and walk up to Cockfield Road in Felsham. Turn right for 70yds and then right into Felsham Hall gateway.

3   Cross the stile on the left and keep direction over three more stiles in quick succession. Bear right along the right hand field edge past the marker post and then with the dyke to the right. Go to the right over a sleeper footbridge and follow this field edge to an earth bridge and turn left over the dyke. Cross the field ahead to a marker post on the left of the tree; this field and several others in this walk may be under cultivation but tracks should be well marked through them, maintain direction over the next field to the hedge.

4   Turn left, go down the field edge with the dyke on the right; carry on through the trees in the corner, past the marker post and along the edge of the next field. Turn left at the hardcore farm road and almost immediate right on a concrete road, cross the stile into the farmyard and bear left past the end of the building. Go right at a marker post down a hedged path, step over the stile and take a left hand diagonal to the footbridge in the corner, cross and turn right along the road.

5   Walk 200yds, past the bird farm and turn right at the signpost. Follow the right hand field edge, with the wide dyke to the right as it bears left; continue general direction through field boundaries to a wooden railed footbridge on the right.

6   Turn right over the bridge and cross the field ahead (a track should be visible) to the right of the corrugated iron barn. Turn right along the farm track and left at the marker post on the obvious path on the left hand field side and continue ahead over the next field. Turn left at the hedge and right at a marker post.

7   Continue on this right hand field edge with the hedge to the right past Monkspark Wood to a five sleeper bridge at the corner. Cross and turn right, follow the edge of the wood to a marker post and turn left over the field to the road. Turn right and walk along the road to the Bradfield Woods car park and your vehicle.

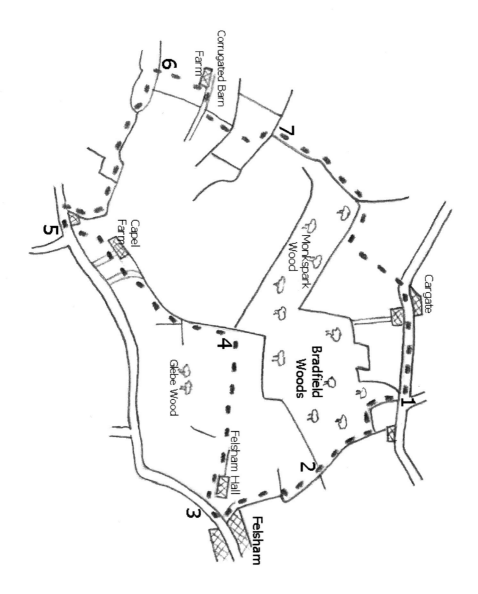

The Blackcap can often be seen in Bradfield and other woodland areas of the walks in this booklet. It is normally a summer visitor, although it sometimes overwinters in this country. The male has a distinctive black cap to its plumage, the female is browner, particularly the underside, but with a red-brown cap instead of black.

There are regular open days in Bradfield Woods featuring demonstrations of woodland crafts.

2   Rede Hole

6 Miles   3 Hours

Park in Rede Village, the 'Plough' pub, no other facilities.

1   Start from the green in front of the 'Plough'. Take the signposted footpath to the left of the Hall along the right hand field edge houses to the right. Turn left in the corner, cross right to the farm track and turn left, continue with the hedge to the right change sides at the marker post through the gap with the hedge now to the left. Keep direction over the fence in the hedge gap on a path through trees.

2   Cross the open field ahead to the hedge corner left of the aeriel, this field may be under cultivation but a track should be well marked through any crop. Continue with the hedge on the left and turn left over a hidden 3 sleeper footbridge. Keep direction towards the aeriel on the right hand field edge through the overgrown gap over the stile and on between the fence and the hedge. Cross the stile and the concrete area and bear right on the narrow concrete road past the aeriel.

3   Turn left down the straight concrete road; after a quarter of a mile bear left at the signpost, take a right hand diagonal through the hedge gap and over the field (track should be visible within any crop). Go through the opening in the fence, bear left through the trees and then bear right over the corner of this next field; go through the hedge gap and turn right along the right hand field edge. Continue through the narrow metal gate and bear right to the right of the pond, go through another gate and bear right on the stony track.

4   Keep going on this farm road, to the right then left around the trees and down to the road at Hawkedon. Turn left, walk up to the signpost and turn right onto the sunken farm road.

5   Turn right along the field edge, turn left in the corner and right at the marker post between the hedge and the barbed wire. Continue through the gate at the end, cross the field and turn left back to the stile/footbridge on the left hand side. Cross and turn right.

6   Carry on up the right hand field edge to the marker post, turn right over the footbridge and through the hedge gap, keep direction upslope on a normally well marked path. Go past two marker posts and through a garden area to the road.

7   Turn left and follow the tarmac farm road past the signpost bearing right, bear left with the road past Francis Farm; keep general direction ahead on an obvious track. Cross the cultivated field ahead to Britton's Farm (a track should be visible within the crop) and walk up to the road, the conifers and the farm to the right.
Completed on the next Page (Eight)

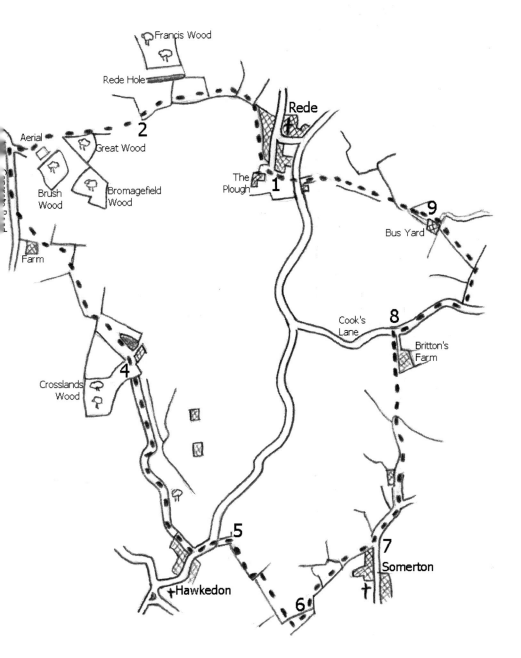

Left of the route between points **2** and **3** approaching the aerial is the highest spot in Suffolk, at 420ft.

24:G

Completion of 2 Rede Hole from the previous Page

8   Follow the road right for a quarter of a mile to a signpost just around a right hand bend, turn left with the dyke to the left up to the marker post and turn left.

9   Keep direction past the end of the bus yard and down the field edge ahead with the dyke to the left. Cross the dyke and continue direction between fields (the dyke starts on the left, 400yds before the road it changes sides). Cross the road and the stile slightly left ahead, follow the right hand field edge right into the corner, go over two awkward stiles/fences back to the village hall.

3   Shaker's Road

5^1/$_4$ Miles   2^1/$_2$ Hours

Park in Barrow, in the car park on the western side of the main road close to the triangular junction. No toilets; shops and pubs close by.

1   Leave the car park and walk across the main road, past the war memorial and over the green signposted to Bury St Edmunds and Saxham. At the signpost on the left, turn left along the tarmac footpath; keep direction over the road, past the garages and up the left hand field edge with the trees to the left. Bear slight left and right, continue on the left hand field edge, go through the hedge lined path next to the cemetery on to the road and turn left.

2   Walk up to the church, turn right and follow the road right at the junction. Go down the slope for two thirds of a mile to the signpost where the road swings left.

3   Turn right along Shaker's Road, the hardcore bridleway and continue with the young trees to the right, through the concrete farmyard to the corner. Turn left past the houses along the road and into the dip.

4   At the signpost take the track right along the field edge with the line of trees to the left. Carry on through the boundary and maintain direction to the road. Turn right up to the crest of the gentle slope.

5   Turn right at the signpost along the path through the trees. As the trees end cross a farm road and continue on the right hand field edge; bear right after 300yds and keep direction through the trees again. Leave on the left hand edge of the field and bear left then right on the right hand field edge. Continue along a tree and hedge lined path past some allotments.

6   At the signpost on the end of the track bear left up to the road and continue right/straight on to the signpost on the far side of Burthorpe Green. Keep direction on the hedge lined path to the road at the houses, turn left along this road to the T-junction. Turn right and follow the roadside path, cross the green and the main road back to the car park and your vehicle.

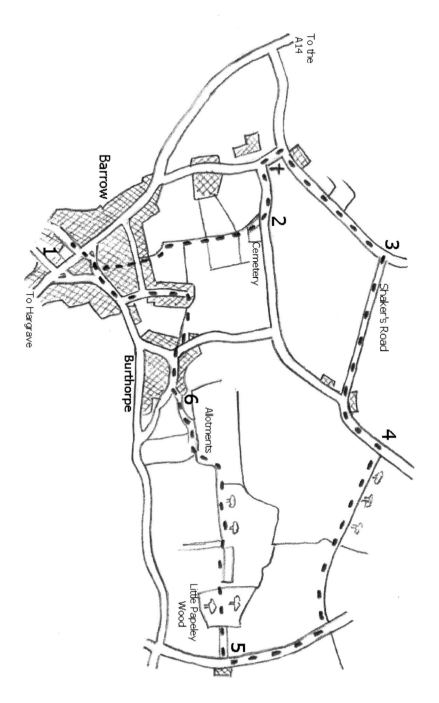

Barrow

To the A14

To Hargave

Burthorpe

Cemetery

Shaker's Road

Allotments

Little Papeley Wood

1

2

3

4

5

6

24:G

4   Baileypool Bridge

5 Miles $2^1/_2$ Hours

Find a parking space in Pakenham. Post Office/shop and pub the 'Fox'. No toilets. Start from the front of the Post Office/shop.

1   Facing away from the shop turn left and walk up to the junction; turn left and follow this road, marked Fen Road after 100yds, to the signpost on the left just past the tractor depot. Keep direction through the trees, over the footbridge and along the access road, go past the marker post and down the hedged path, still at the back of the houses.

2   At an overgrown signpost marked with a 2, turn right through the hedge gap and walk up the track parallel to the telegraph poles. Cross the farm road and keep direction on the right hand field edge with the hedge to the right. At the next farm road left then immediate right past the signpost still on the right hand field edge. Go past the trees and follow the path left then right between fence and pond.

3   Turn right along the tarmac farm road, go between the farm buildings and straight ahead down the wide hedged, grassy path. At the marker post turn right along the left hand field edge to the next marker post and cross left over the stile. Take the track ahead over the field and the sleeper bridge/stile. Turn left up to the marker post and turn right along the track with the dyke to the right up to the road.

4   Follow the road left to the second junction at the green triangle and turn right. As the road swings left over Baileypool Bridge, go straight on along the bridleway and carry on with the hedge to the left up to the corner. Turn left through the hedge gap and continue with the trees to the right through the gap in the corner.

5   Cross the field bearing away from the reservoir past the telegraph pole on a track which should be visible within any crop. At the corner ahead, go past the marker post and cross the stile; carry on ahead up the right hand field edge over the next stile, turn left and follow the edge of the field to the road at Bull Bridge.

6   Continue straight on along the flinty bridleway and bear right, around the back of the farm buildings. Carry on ahead on the less substantial track with the hedge and the dyke to the right, through the hedge gap to the corner of Pakenham Wood.

7   Fork right and follow the track with the trees to the left to the junction of paths at the hidden signpost no 7; turn left along the path through the wood. At the end of the trees turn right with the trees to the right. From the corner go straight on through the trees, continue between fields and pass through the kissing gate. Cross the meadow straight on down to the road at the junction in Pakenham and go into the village to find your vehicle.

24:

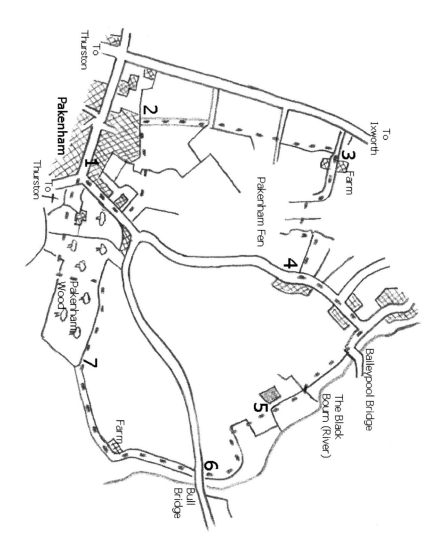

Pakenham boasts both a windmill and a watermill within its boundaries although both are physically closer to Ixworth village. A watermill has existed on the site since Norman times, the present building replaced a Tudor watermill in the 18th century and is open for visitors on certain days during the summer.

24:G

boundary, cross through the hedge gap to the right and carry on so that the hedge is still to the left. Keep along the field edge up to the metal gate and bear left to the road. Turn right along the road for just over a third of a mile.

3 In the small settlement of Bird's End turn left at the signpost, through the wide metal gate and follow the path through the trees. Cross the footbridge and keep on the right hand field edge bearing left to the top corner. Go over the two-sleeper footbridge and turn right along the field edge to the marker post. Transfer sides over the footbridge and carry on direction with the hedge now to the left.

4 Pass through the gap in the corner and follow this field edge to the right, cross the footbridge and continue past the marker post upslope on the right hand field edge. Bear right and go ahead through the hedge gap, over the footbridge and keep direction along the enclosed path into Hargrave. Turn right for 150yds, then left at the signpost past the village hall and up to the marker post.

5 Turn left; go through the trees and the metal kissing gate. The path goes from here to the opposite fence and then back within this same field to the corner on the right with the unusual iron stile/fence. Cross and follow the path directly ahead parallel with the telegraph poles, this field may be under cultivation but the track should

be well marked. Cross the footbridge and bear left, turn right in the corner and almost immediate left over a stile/footbridge. Turn right; step over a tricky stile, the next stile and along the field edge past the wood, Coldtrench Plantation.

6 Cross the footbridge in the corner and follow the field edge left. At the junction in front of the trees, fork right, walk past the wood, Carter's Park, to the marker post at the far corner and turn right. Turn left then right at marker posts on this field edge and then left at the next junction on the green path between fields. Carry on to the road, turn right and walk up to the T-junction.

Completed on the next Page (Fourteen)

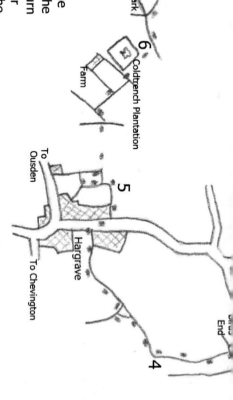

Carter's Park
6
Coldtrench Plantation
Farm
To Ousden
5
Hargrave
To Chevington
End
4

5 Castle Holes

$4^1/_2$ Hours

$9^3/_4$ Miles

Park in Barrow, in the car park on the western side of the main road close to the triangular junction.
No toilets; shops and pubs close by.

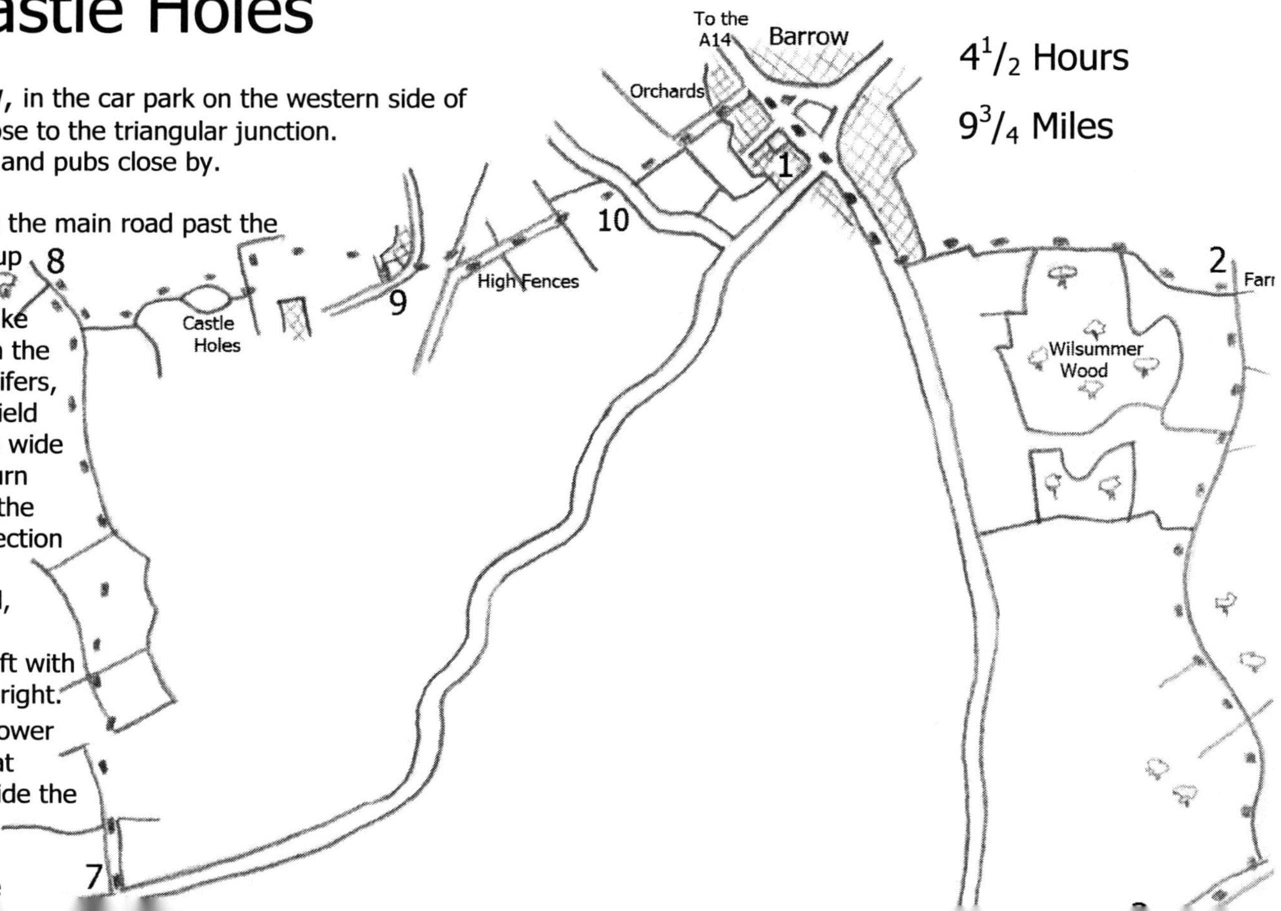

1 Turn right up the main road past the junctions. Walk up to the signpost on the left and take the path between the dyke and the conifers, continue on the field edge through the wide hedge gap and turn right then left at the corner. Keep direction into the trees of Wilsummer Wood, as the trees end bear right then left with the hedge to the right.

2 Just before Lower Farm, turn right at a junction alongside the dyke with the trees to the left; continue over the

Completion of 5 Castle Holes from the previous page

7   Go straight on along the bridleway ahead. At a marker post at a hedge gap take a right hand diagonal over the field; a track should be visible within any crop and cross the wide bridge in the far corner.

8   Continue direction to the marker post just short of the wood, turn right through the gap and double back along the other side of the hedge to the corner. Turn left and bear slight left then right, around the moats of Castle Holes through the gate near the house. Bear left along the top of the field to the marker post and turn right downslope through the gate near the garage. Turn right to the driveway.

9   Turn left and go down to the metal signpost (marked Barrow on the other side) and bear right through the high metal gate. Turn right in front of the next high gate, walk between high fences and turn sharp left uphill; continue through a last high gate. Cross the footbridge and keep direction over the field (a track should be visible), crossing the sleeper bridge halfway, to the signpost at the hedge gap in the corner.

10   Cross the road and carry on along the right hand field edge over the footbridge and up the fenced path. Continue through the cul-de-sac to the main road in Barrow. Turn right past the ponds back to the car park and your vehicle.

6   Tan Office Green

5 Miles   2¹/₄ Hours

Find a parking space near the village hall on Tan Office Green; there may be space on the side of the road next to the hedge near the hall. No facilities.

1   Facing away from the village hall next to the Chevington sign turn left, follow the roadside paths to Depden Lane and turn right; after 120yds turn right into Tan Office Lane and carry on past the footpath sign and the metal gate. As this farm road bears right turn left at a signpost through a narrow gap.

2   Turn right along the right hand field edge and bear right through a wider hedge gap. Turn left along the track keeping the original direction with the hedge now to the left. Go through the gateway ahead, turn right, left and right around the inset corner; follow this field edge with the stream to the right all the way to the road.

3   Turn right for 30yds, bear left at the signpost through the gap and down the right hand field edge keeping the original direction with the stream still to the right. Cross the stream at the footbridge, turn left to the corner and then right up the slope with the hedge to the left. Turn left through the gap at the corner downslope with the hedge now right; turn right through a narrow gap at a marker post.

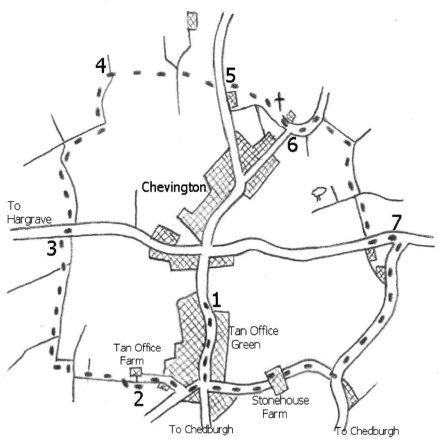

Chevington

To Hargrave

Tan Office Farm

Tan Office Green

Stonehouse Farm

To Chedburgh

To Chedburgh

4 Cross the narrow footbridge and continue over the field ahead, a track should be visible within any crop, go through the hedge gap and bear slight right over the next field keeping the three solitary trees to the left. Walk into the corner and cross the three sleeper bridge in the gap. Bear right over this field, a track should be well marked towards the house. Go through the gap and cross the road.

5 Pass by the signpost left of the house and follow the right hand field edge; cross over an almost hidden stile to the right. Go up this narrow field and step over the stile to the left, bear right and turn immediate left through a hedge gap. Turn right along the path between the gravestones and go through the gate beyond All Saints Church; continue on the short piece of tarmac road.

6 Turn left through the wooden gates in the corner and carry on down the tarmac drive. Before the cottages on the left are reached, turn sharp right up the sloping entrance to a field. Continue on the left hand field edge with the hedge to the left, follow the hedge right and at the top of the rise keep direction on the right hand field edge up to the road. Turn left down to the T-junction.

Completed on the next Page (Sixteen)

7   Turn right, signposted Chedburgh, and walk for half a mile to a gateway on the right marked only by the remains of an arrow on the right hand gatepost. Turn right and follow this grass path between fields, continue past the left hand end of the white farmhouse at Stonehouse Farm and bear right along the tarmac road to the junction. Turn right along Tan Office Green to find your vehicle.

7   Eastlow Hill

$4^3/_4$ Miles $2^1/_2$ Hours

Park at Rougham Church in the lay-by on the opposite side of the road. Grid ref. TL911627. No facilities.

1   Leave the lay-by through the narrow footpath exit, cross the road and take the footpath signposted towards the church. Turn right in front of the church and go through the gate ahead. Keep direction along the left hand edge of the school field through the kissing gate and the left hand edge of the next two larger fields.

2   Turn left over the footbridge at the marker post in the corner; after 200yds turn right at the marker post and walk up to the road. Maintain direction on left hand field edges, to the footbridge/stile on the left 50yds from the corner. Cross and turn right over the stile in the corner, take a slight left through the marked gate and the gateway ahead between metal barriers. Bear slight left and step over the stile next to the metal gate right of the pond, on to the road.

3   Turn right for 40yds along the road to the signpost on the right, and cross the stile on the left; continue slight right over the stile. Carry on ahead over this field and cross the marked footbridge. Go over the drive; bear right past a marker post, straight on over two stiles and continue alongside the wicket fence to the road.

4   Walk down the road to the left for 175yds to the signpost opposite the junction and turn left. Keep direction on a winding path through the trees. Carry on along left hand field edges and over the footbridges with the hedge and the dyke to the left, for half a mile. Continue to the marker post next to the signpost (there is no footbridge over the dyke crossing ahead and no arrow or sign pointing right).

5   Turn right down the left hand field edge and the farm track past the kink to the marker post, turn left through the wide hedge gap. Go down the right hand edge of this field, turn left in the corner and continue to the end of the hedge. Turn right with the trees to the left up to the hardcore farm road.

6   Take the short track to the left and carry on up the left hand field edge, at the top turn right and walk up to the signpost. Go left over the sloping footbridge and follow the field edge parallel to the telegraph poles.   Just past the overhead wires change sides of the hedge and continue between the hedge and the trees. Bear right then left along the wide hardcore track to a signpost on the left.

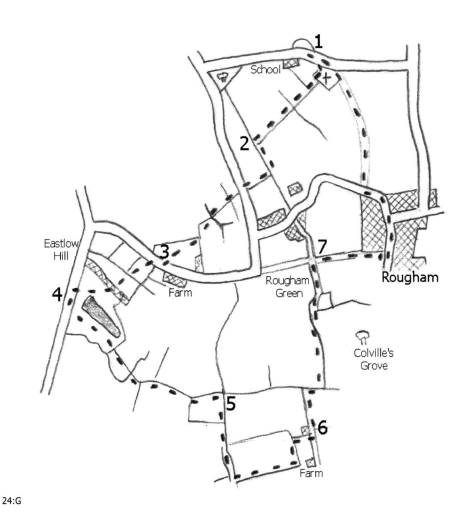

School
Eastlow Hill
3
4
Farm
Rougham Green
7
Rougham
Colville's Grove
5
6
Farm

2

1

24:G

7 Turn right through the hedge gap down the path on the left hand field edge; keep on this track past the bungalows to the road in the main part of Rougham. Turn left along this road and follow it left. After 150yds turn right past the wooden barriers along a tarmac path. Carry on up this path to the road at the church and turn left back to the lay-by and your vehicle.

8 Barrow Green

5$\frac{1}{2}$ Miles   2$\frac{3}{4}$ Hours

Park in Barrow, in the car park on the western side of the main road close to the triangular junction. No toilets, shops, takeaway food and pubs close by.

1   Leave the car park, go back to the main road and turn left, walk past the shop and both ponds and turn left into Orchard Farm Barns. Continue from the left hand corner on the enclosed path, with the orchard to the right. Cross the footbridge and keep direction on the left hand field edge to the road.

2   Bear left over the field ahead which may be under cultivation although a track should be visible within any crop, cross the sleeper footbridge and continue direction over the next field. Go over the footbridge, through the high gate and continue between the high fences; at the bottom of the slope turn right. Turn left through another gate and bear left upslope.

3   Go through the gate behind the adjacent garage and carry on upslope with the fence to the right, to the marker post at the top. Bear left into the narrow field corner near the house and pass through this gate, walk along the enclosed path right of Denham Castle (Castle Holes on OS maps). Keep on this field edge to the line of trees at the far left corner.

4   Turn right along the field edge with the trees to the left and turn left through the kissing gate. Keep ahead and turn right on the track with the trees to the left, continue to the tarmac road. Take this road right, through the farmyard and turn right past the black barn up to the signpost by the cottages.

5   Fork right down the concrete road past the cottages into the dip. Keep straight on, over the slope and into the next dip; cross the footbridge and bear right to the road.

6   Cross and continue ahead, past the signpost, between the hedge and the wire fence, carry on over a substantial sleeper footbridge, uphill on a left hand field edge with the hedge on the left, into the far left corner. Cross the footbridge/stile slightly to the right. Take a slight right hand diagonal over the field to a stile in the opposite fence, close to a bungalow. Cross the stile here and walk straight over the lawn to the road.

7   Turn right for 300yds to the signpost and turn left along the track through the trees to the field; carry on along the right hand field edge to the road. Turn left along the roadside path to the church and turn right signposted Risby.

8   Walk up to the signpost for Barrow Green and turn right along the hedged path with the cemetery to the left. Continue on the right hand field edge to the playing

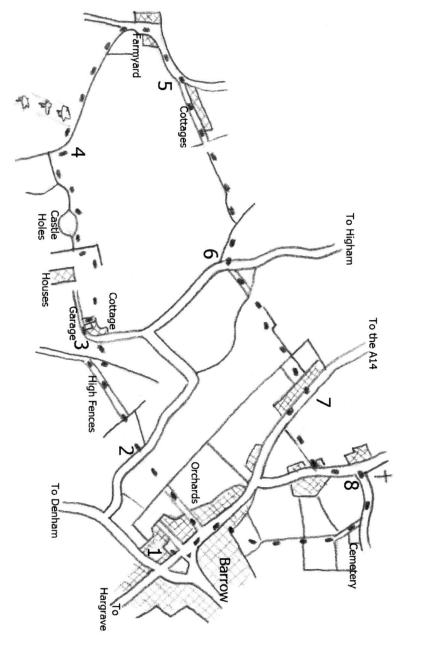

field, bear right past the swings and exit through the village hall car park. Turn left to the junction at the village sign close to the car park and your vehicle.

1 Bear left out of the entrance and go straight on at the roundabout, cross this busy road (A134) when possible and continue direction on the opposite roadside path. Keep direction right of the next roundabout up Beech Rise past the cul-de-sac sign. Turn right in the corner through the posts and left along the footpath with the brick wall then the fence to the left. Carry on across a crossroads of paths over the access road and up to the T-junction, turn left over the A1302 (deceptively busy).

2 On the other side continue direction and bear left at the junction. Walk along the tarmac path between hedges with Holywater Meadows to the right, up to the houses. Maintain direction uphill between the houses, over the busier road and straight on between trees past the hospital.

3 In the top corner turn left with the wire fence to the left and then right on the wide track through the trees; bear left on the path through the gap and right on the track over the grass keeping nearer to the houses than the trees. Go through the gateway in the corner and follow the right hand field edge as it bears right. Walk along the path through the trees to the signpost.

4 Go straight across the field ahead which may be under cultivation but a track should be well marked within any crop. Bear right at the clump of trees surrounding

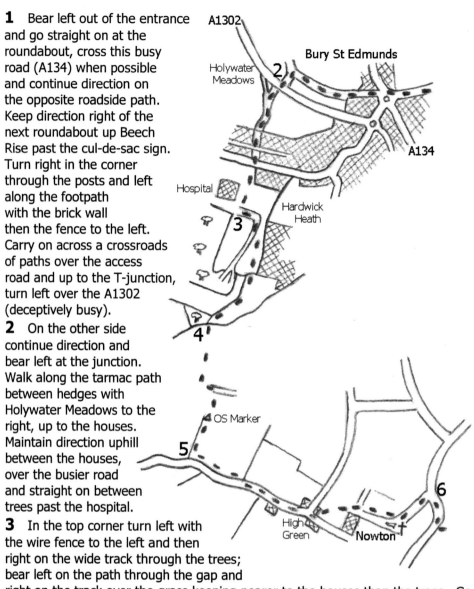

Completed on the next Page (Twenty Two)

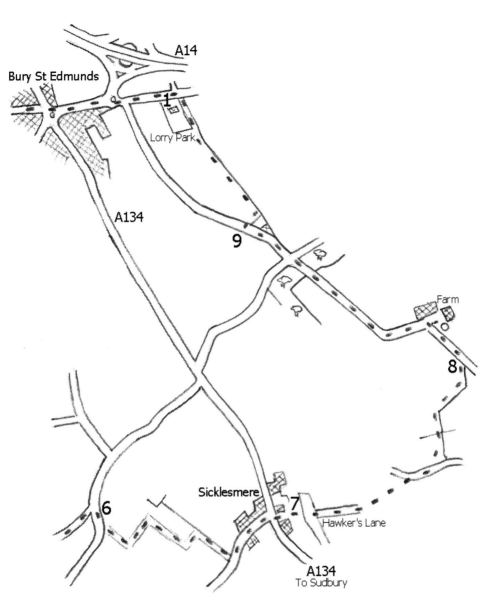

9 Hawker's Lane

$7^3/_4$ Miles $\qquad$ $3^3/_4$ Hours

Park in the lorry park signposted from the eastern junction off the A14 to Bury St Edmunds. Toilets and transport café.

the pond and then immediate left with the dyke to the left. Turn left over the sleeper bridge and right to regain direction past the Ordnance Survey Pillar; follow the right hand field edge to the road.

5 Turn left along the right hand field edge and then the road; go straight on at the junction into High Green. After 75yds turn left over a stile and walk diagonally over the field to the stile at the opposite corner. Cross this stile and the one ahead at the far end of the barn, keep direction over the road and the next field to the church. Bear left along the road to the junction and turn right.

6 Walk uphill to the signpost and turn left. Follow the footpath and turn left at the corner, turn right at the marker post along the line of trees, follow the track left and right again at the marker post downhill to the road. Turn left and walk into the village of Sicklesmere. At the A134 turn right over the bridge, cross the road and bear slight right past the front of the 'Rushbrooke Arms'; continue up the steps past the picnic tables and through the fence gap.

7 Go straight over the field ahead and uphill along Hawker's Lane, the path between the trees. At the end bear left on a normally well trimmed path through the grass; continue ahead/right on the farm road and take the path diagonally left (with the pond on the left) before the road kinks right. Go past the marker post and along the field edge with the trees to the right, continue right then left on this track with the hedge still to the right to a concrete farm road and turn left.

8 Walk up to the farm and turn left along the farm road, bear right at the corner with the line of trees and walk down to the road at a T-junction. Go straight on down Rushbrooke Lane, follow the road left round the corner to a signpost.

9 Turn right down the edge of the dyke to another signpost, turn left on the right hand field edge and keep direction; continue through the hedge lined path to the road at the front of the lorry park. Turn left to the gate and your vehicle inside.

10   Rougham Downs

4 Miles   1³/₄ Hours

Park at **Rougham Church** in the lay-by on the opposite side of the road. Grid ref. TL911627. No facilities.

1 Go to the exit end of the lay-by, turn left through the kissing gate and walk ahead between the avenue of trees. Out of the trees continue with the fence to the right over a stile and along a short piece of road nearly to the A14.

24:G

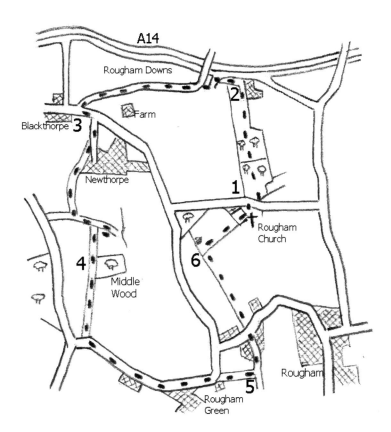

2   Take the concrete road left, parallel to the dual carriageway and follow it left past the aerial, bear right over the hump and left through the metal gates. Keep going along this concrete road past Rougham Downs all the way to Blackthorpe.

3   At the gate turn left for 300yds and right into Mouse Lane. Walk up to the RUPP signpost and bear right along the field edge at the back of the houses of Newthorpe. Keep going ahead up the often overgrown track between hedges to a T-junction with a wider track. Turn left, (note the hedge gap on the right!) the track bears right, ending at a junction of field entrances, turn right along the field edge parallel to the path just walked, to the track left going past the young trees.

4   Continue past Middle Wood to the road. Turn left and walk into Rougham Green. As the road turns sharp left go straight on along the stony then grass track.

5   Turn left at the signpost and follow this hardcore track back to the road, keep direction over the road, footbridge and stile. Continue ahead on the left hand field edge over another stile/footbridge and under the overhead wires to the corner.

Completed on the next Page (Twenty Four)

Completion of **10** Rougham Downs from the previous Page

6 Cross the footbridge and turn right along the field edge, go through the boundary and the kissing gate. Carry on along the edge of the school field into the churchyard. Turn left at the church, up the gravel path and across the road to the lay-by and your vehicle.

The Walking Close to series in Eastern England

The Norfolk Broads (Northern Area)
Epping Forest
The Colne near Colchester
The Cam and the Granta near Cambridge
The Orwell near Ipswich
Clare, Cavendish and Haverhill
The Stour near Sudbury
The Norfolk Broads (Southern Area)
The Nene near Peterborough
North West Norfolk (Hunstanton and Wells)
The Nene near Oundle
The Great Ouse near King's Lynn
The Nene near Northampton
The Great Ouse north of Milton Keynes
South Lincolnshire
North Norfolk (Cromer and Sheringham)
Aldeburgh, Snape and Thorpeness
Southwold and the Suffolk Coast
The Lincolnshire Wolds (North)
The Lincolnshire Wolds (South)
The Welland near Stamford
Bourne and the Deepings
The Great Ouse in Huntingdonshire

Newmarket
Lavenham
Dedham Vale
Grafham Water
Thetford Forest
Stowmarket
Woburn Abbey
Lincoln
Rutland Water
The Isle of Ely

The Walking Close to series in the South and South West

Chichester
Exmouth
Romsey
Shaftesbury
Cheddar Gorge

Salisbury and Stonehenge
The South Devon Coast
Winchester
Blandford Forum
Glastonbury and Wells